THE QUIET POOL

*Fly Fishing the Rivers and Still Waters
of Washington*

THE QUIET POOL

*Fly Fishing the Rivers and Still Waters
of Washington*

Dan Homel

*Foreword & epilogue by JM Hurlbert
illustrated by Ariel Shimondle*

Forrest - Park Publishers
Bellingham, Washington

Forrest Park Publishers
P.O. Box 29775
Bellingham, Washington
98228-1775
(360) 647-2505

PRINTED IN THE UNITED STATES OF AMERICA

ISBN: 1-879522-04-7

CREDITS

Cover Art ~ R. Van Demark
Transparency for separations ~ Mark Bergsma
Electronic pre-press ~ Marcus Yearout
Illustrations ~ Ariel Shimondle
PMT ~ Quicksilver Photo Lab

Photographs
Black & White ~ Ralph Wahl
Color ~ D.B. Homel

Special Thanks to ~ J.M. Hurlbert, Richard and Diane Van Demark, Harold Jellison, Ralph Wahl, Errol McWhirk, Lyle Hand, Chico Peters, Dick Thompson, Deb Cicchitti, Rick Hafele, Dwight Lyons, Peter Mills, Ed Ruckey, Ariel Shimondle, Jan, Joe, Will and Atessa Homel, Mom and Dad, The U.S. Forest Service at Mt. St. Helens, The Fourth Corner Fly Fishers.

Front Cover ~ *The Methow River* in pastel by R. Van Demark.

Back Cover ~ *A Brace of Cutthroat* (Wahl, Skagit River). Lower photos D.B. Homel.

To my bros.
Kevin, Jeff and Steve

Table of Contents

Introduction

The Quiet Pool is my effort, in concert with several talented artists and creative minds, to convey the essence and spirit of Northwest fly fishing in story form.

All found here is non-fiction, with the exception of "The Poacher." And that tale is based on a combined series of true events.

Our challenge and goal in developing this book was, first and foremost, to stimulate thought. It is my hope that, at least, a chapter or paragraph within serves to motivate other anglers to explore new destinations with the fly rod and, to form a covenant with their favorite fishery resource. That pact being a commitment to help preserve habitat upon which the perpetuation of native species depends.

Most experienced fly fishers already know of this natural treasure, but we all need to be reminded now and then. I, for one, do — as the majority of my days are spent behind a desk, waiting in a line, or paying bills.

Luckily, fly fishing in the beautiful (and now much too alluring) State of Washington gives us a chance to step-back and look at things in a different way. To recreate — this is the gift of angling.

Pass the gift on to another, especially our youth, and the future will be brimming with responsible, enlightened *afishionados*.

D.B. Homel
Whatcom County
Bellingham, Washington

Foreword

by J.M. Hurlbert

Everyone has his or her path to that primal ground of our being, nature's lair. Dan Homel's path, like the muddy path so many of us slip and stumble down, swatting madly at mosquitoes, cursing and battling underbrush for possession of our gear, has always led to water; water and the life that there lurks, sneering arrogantly at our frenzied attempts to weave some small part of our lives into the pattern of nature. Fly fishing has a special way of facilitating this essential link. It tends to become a lifetime obsession, this search for that certain keyway into the mystery of nature; that line sometimes cast crookedly at the core of one's soul - that is, when it is not snarled in some fly-eating root ball while we pratfall in the shallows. When it all comes together, when we are in "synch" with the currents we are graced with what Dan calls the "touch" (not to be confused with the similar term "touched" by which fly fishers are so often referred to by spouses and other insensitive associates!). Few other activities demand that we be so in tune with our environment to succeed and few exist that can so regularly humble and humiliate us when, by nature's caprice or our own myopic lack of insight and understanding, we find ourselves stumbling drunkenly over our own ignorance and foolishness. One way or another we always come out of our angling encounters "touched" by mother nature.

As Dan well illustrates, the camaraderie and obsession of those who share the nostalgic lore, the wonder and angst (known by the unsympathetic as nonsense, confusion and irritation) of fly fishing is an added benefit of our sport. Fly fishing is a process best shared. A never ending project that provides a never ending source of mysteries to be investigated, debated, explored, hoarded and shared. The varieties and pedigrees of the gear alone, as you will read, is enough to keep one opinionated, argumentative and bankrupt for a lifetime! Even among the most solitary types there are almost always a few boon companions with whom to share and argue the experiences and memories of the sport. Dan shares in these pages his own boon companionship in the memories and musings of time spent on the water.

J. Marc Hurlbert

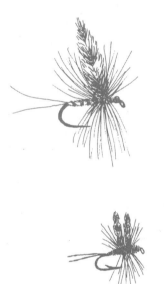

Sloughs along the Skagit

Sea-run coastal cutthroat trout are, perhaps, the most easily caught of all anadromous fish in the Puget Sound region. The
term *anadromous*, describes the inherent characteristic of a fish species to migrate up-river,
after a period of time in saltwater, for the purpose
of spawning. All species of the scientific family
Salmonidae can follow this trait, including the
coastal cutthroat, migratory rainbow trout (steelhead) and the Pacific salmons (coho, chinook,
pink, and chum).

A bold distinction separates the familiar coho
or chinook (king) salmon from the cutthroat
trout. Unlike a salmon, the migrating cutthroat
may not die after spawning and can return to the
river of birth two or more times as a natural prog-
enitor of it's strain.

Habitat destruction and their aforementioned propensity to be fooled by bait, lure or fly, are both factors accounting for the demise of a once great sea-run cutthroat fishery. A fishery almost entirely dedicated to the sport angler and heavily reliant upon natural propagation as opposed to the hatchery generated existence currently imposed upon the majority of our steelhead and salmon.

However, there is hope yet for this truly wild trout; first acknowledged in a journal of the Lewis and Clark expedition in 1805, but long before that a perennial fixture in the culture of the ancient indigenous people of it's native range.

Despite the onslaught of plunkers, drifters and fly casters, who in the past seemed to share a feeling of indifference to the trout's plight, the cutthroat are making a valiant comeback. Northwest residents miss the colorful little trout traveling upstream during October and out-migrating in the April rains. These precious gems of inestimable value are no longer ... "just another fish to be thrown in the ice chest". Many rivers, tributaries, and minor streams, ultimately flowing to the salt chuck, are now restricted with no-kill regulations. These laws, without question, foster positive direction for the species' renewal.

My best fall days have been spent in pursuit of the coastal cutthroat. The fish return to their home waters from a journey along beaches and estuaries, never venturing too far from familiar shores. And I try to intercept them at some point up-stream in the venue of their summer haunts.

A traditional destination has become the narrow, meandering sloughs of the Skagit River, northeast of Mt. Vernon, Washington. One area of the river, in particular, consumes my thoughts from late September on into early October. We call it the Amazon. And it is every bit a rain forest, maybe not in the scientific sense, but how one is struck by it's dripping, soggy nature. I invade it's sanctuary just once a season.

A hike-in is required to reach the slough, over a slippery carpet of decayed maple leaves and oozing slugs. Snarled, fallen alder branches cause abrupt detours in route, but this only adds to the adventure.

Upon reaching the clearing this year, I was full of anticipation as a light rain began to fall. A dramatic mist enveloped the setting. Had the river swollen and muddied so that it would be impossible to present a fly? Of course, I would fish anyway. Were the trout too far up-stream? It was already mid-October.

My companion on this excursion happened to be the irrepressible Richard Van Demark, a veteran Washington angler of remarkable skill. In fact, it was Dick who introduced me to this exact location. Today we had carried float tubes through the tangled deciduous jungle, intending to cross the slough and fish in some niches and rip-rap not otherwise accessible by ordinary wading tactics. Sitting in the inflated tubes, we hoped also to fin our way up-stream as the current allowed.

Soon we were fastened into all the necessary gear and I glanced over to a spot on the far bank. A spot that a few years before had been occupied by a good friend who had since moved south to the big city. I remembered that he had taken several nice cutthroat there on his favorite dry fly, a Royal Wulff — named for the originator, Lee Wulff, pioneer fly fisher who coined the phrase "... a trout is too important to be caught only once ..." many years before conservation was fashionable.

It was good holding water for sea-runs, with a cut bank that extended for some distance before it disappeared into a densely treed precipice.

Preferring hairwing streamers to the dry fly, I tied on an attractor pattern remotely resembling a stubby salmon fry. A primary material to the fly's construction is pink rabbit fur. Presumably, due to the coloration, trout mistake it for a salmon egg as well. These small artificials are tied on a size 12 wet fly hook, produced by Partridge of England. This excellent, sharp hook provides adequate weight to slowly and carefully sink the fly amongst numerous snags encountered in the slough.

I was able to wade to the spot, dragging my float tube behind and then securing it to the bank. My first cast was off-target. The leader landed in a clump and was soon carried-off by current drag. It seemed more efficient to maneuver in-close to the bank and simply "dap" my fly in against the vegetation. "Dapping" (or dabbling) is an old European method whereby the rod is merely extended way out, with the fly line plopped into the water at that position. Nothing fancy, and no cast.

The idea paid off. As the fly sank, a slow lift of the rod tip produced a solid strike. I was very aware of the assortment of snags protruding from the bank into the water, so the trout was not allowed much line. Fingering the reel spool provided controlled pressure until I could raise the fish to within reach. The light leader held! My hands gently cradled a beautiful, hook jawed male of about nineteen inches. He may have been in fresh water for some time, since a bright red slash-mark appeared clearly below the jaw. This distinguishing feature or "cut-throat" is not always visible on fresh, sea-run adult fish.

I reclaimed my fly and urged the trout back into the slough. My trance was broken by a splash, as Dick rose one to the dry fly. It was a silvery hen-fish somewhat smaller than mine. He had been fishing a short distance away in a side channel of lower, clear water. Before I joined him there, he had caught and released another.

It was time to think about moving up-current in the tubes, so we decided to first take a lunch break and make the final preparations. Dick paused to reflect on the changes that had taken place in this section of the Skagit drainage, a throughway for tremendous winter steelhead runs and salmon migrations including the prolific pink salmon (humpy) in odd numbered years. A few crude, old fishing shacks still remained beside modern development. But the car ferry-rafts, seven of them, which decades ago provided access to this side of the river, are a faint recollection passed-on from old timers to a new generation not always interested in history.

A few miles from our picnic spot was the former location of a famous log jam pool where early fly fishing innovators Ralph Wahl, Les Townley, and Judge Olsen plied the Skagit for winter steelhead. In those days (1935 - 1960), anglers were challenged to keep their flies below the surface within the steelhead's zone of view. The weather was often a handicap in January, when icy winds and blowing snow caused rod guides to freeze and reels to fail. Nevertheless, these rugged men captured many *Field & Stream* fishing contest award winners in the rainbow trout category. And they did so without the sophisticated tackle available today. Waxed silk lines, hand-tied leaders, crude make-shift wire stripping baskets, and heavy bamboo rods made fishing more difficult than it would be for the modern angler.

The article <u>Winter Steelheads on Flies</u> authored by Ralph Wahl appeared in the February, 1943 issue of *Field & Stream.* It is probably one of the earliest magazine pieces on the subject and includes a fascinating description of Ralph's first encounter with a fly caught winter fish.

Ralph Wahl spent a good part of his leisure time recording these great fish in a pristine environment on black and white film. In this way Ralph was able to express his feelings for the river, and the wildlife so dependent upon it. His wonderful books allow us a glimpse of what he saw.

Now, the river is different. Ralph's log jam pool is gone. The fish are not nearly so abundant. But they are still here, and so are the bald eagles, great blue herons, deer and maybe, in more remote corners of the headwaters, cougar, black bear and wolf. From it's beginnings in British Columbia the Skagit survives and surprisingly thrives, compared to other watersheds so close to a burgeoning populous.

Then abruptly, our thoughts were of the present. The slough was rising with increased precipitation. If we were to utilize the tubes to gain access to the upper reaches, time was of the essence.

Upon entering the water we found the current to be relentless. We were forced to pull ourselves along by grabbing the side of the bank. This slow progress continued for what seemed to be an hour. Finally, after moving up-stream only 75 yards, I let-go and began floating back down to our launching point. I was traveling quickly and could not execute a cast, so our experiment with the float tubes was a bust.

Suddenly, a large salmon of about twenty

pounds leaped clear over my lap and I lunged backward, almost capsizing the tube! As cold water flooded into my waders, Dick chuckled — he was directly behind me and had seen the whole embarrassing incident.

No more pensive reflections. All I could think about now was a dry shirt and hot coffee in the truck. We followed our own tracks on the return hike through the "jungle", and I met with no further mishaps, other than the expected slug slime on the bottom of my boots.

After loading our gear, Dick negotiated a rough dirt road toward the main river-side drive. On the way, we stopped the truck to watch a bulldozer, bogged down while excavating for another foundation; another change in the landscape and, a new step in the transformation away from the primitive area as it was in the day of Ralph and the Judge.

I suppose most things are altered with time; things fall apart, and we must adapt or accept change to some degree. But just imagine how it was. Catching the car-ferry, crossing the Skagit and knowing that when you returned weeks later, year after year — no one else would have touched the place.

The old bulldozer groaned and smoked and

sunk deeper into the ground, thick mud forging a temporary defense against the assault on history. Finally, as it gained traction, the machine turned sharply and lurched forward — a rusty knife in the back of paradise.

Desert Oasis

The desert country of south central and eastern Washington is a regional anomaly — particularly in the eye of the tourist, drawn to the Pacific Northwest by visions of towering old growth forests and rain-drenched, rocky beaches. A vast expanse of terrain, known as the Columbia Basin, is fully desert in this state. Curiously, here is where some of our trout grow the largest.

Several factors contribute to this desert angling phenomena, not the least of which is a low density of human population. Credit is certainly due the Washington Department of Fish and Wildlife, an agency both cursed and praised by a wide variety of organizations and clubs — all lobbying for their own special interests.

But the fact remains; there exists one of the finest trout fishing arenas in the world right in our own backyard (or within a days drive of Seattle).

The genius behind the exceptional desert lake fishing in Washington is the "Quality Waters" program. The State utilizes a combination of special and selective regulations including catch-and-release, low limits, size limits, fly-fishing-only, and bait prohibition. In this way each lake is managed individually for maximum potential. Nevertheless, the main ingredient to the Quality Waters Program is a superior strain of rainbow trout broodstock. Their progeny are planted as tiny fingerlings (fry) which balloon to catchable size in a years time or twenty inches in three years.

The growth environment is ideal in the desert lakes, which provide a rich habitat for aquatic insects, a primary source of trout food. Comparable rainbow trout fry plants have been a disappointment in western Washington lowland lakes where variables such as bird predation, disease loss, and slower growth due to lower lake productivity have hampered efforts in establishing similar programs. A preponderance of western lakes are, therefore, a "put-and-take" show with very few large, carry-over rainbows. Each year millions of ten to twelve inch fish are stocked and then killed within months — a grand scheme designed to supply license holders with traditional opening day recreation.

So, in search of serious trouting, we of the Puget Sound must travel east of the mountains to partake of a great bounty. A fishery that is sometimes so good that one can be nearly spoiled by entire days and nights of torrid action. Big fish; leader stretching, hook-bending, reel screaming four pounders and acrobatic, unpredictable, bright seventeen inchers.

Yet often, fishing can go sour. The sky darkens, the wind blows, and it rains horizontally. Casting a fly or lure becomes dangerous, and discomfort usually leads the angler back to tent, camper or car.

This can be harsh, foreboding land. Arid, dry-hot in the summer and teeth-chattering cold in the winter. It comes as no surprise that the landscape of basalt cliffs and native shrub steppe vegetation is called a "scabland". But, let us not be deceived. Amidst this unlikely backdrop is the unusual collection of lakes, marshes, and ponds.

Many of the desert lakes were actually formed as a result of seepage from irrigation waters necessary to the fertility of nearby, expansive fields of wheat and alfalfa, important crops of the region. Ancient, dry coulees or sandy depressions left by erosion and flood have been filled with life giving waters to form true oases supporting a diverse culture of plants and animals. Commonly observed in these unique wet areas are diving goldeneye ducks and the colorful red-winged or yellow-headed blackbirds. Western painted turtles and muskrat swim near shoreline sedge grasses. And rarely seen, but very active during the cover of night are the elusive coyotes. Measure your footsteps carefully here — rattlesnakes are abundant.

And then there are the trout. Magnificent rainbows (*Oncorhynchus mykiss*) in most lakes, along with some browns.

The brown trout is a species offering great thermotolerance, being able to withstand water temperatures as high as 75 degrees. Accordingly, browns may be a viable option for future fry plantings in lakes where eutrophication has occurred. Eutrophication can mark a significant change in water quality and temperature, and is the result of nutrient enrichment caused by human induced deforestation, consequent erosion, and siltation. It is not necessarily a word of doom, but it is an imminent condition of fresh water ecology to be reckoned with by all who appreciate clear, cold still-waters.

Select lakes of high alkaline content are planted with lahonton cutthroat trout, gigantic but rather lethargic creatures. Washington's lahontons are the offspring of eggs obtained from Nevada's Summit Lake Stock. The native range of these fish also includes Pyramid Lake, Walker Lake, Lake Tahoe, and the Truckee River Drainage in California and Nevada (all part of prehistoric Lake Lahonton). Lahonton cutthroat have the ability to survive in lakes once barren of fish life. When planted in alkaline desert waters such as Lake Lenore, in Grant County, lahontons grow fat on the green *Gammarus* shrimp found there in large numbers.

But it is the rainbow that is clearly most significant in desert lakes; and they are a very handsome trout. As the name suggests, they exhibit a pallet of colors; from glowing silver sides to green at the back with a white underbelly. A subdued pink or red ribbon runs from behind gill-cover to caudal (tail) fin. Spotting can be faint and irregular to leopard-skin vivid on some specimens. Each one is a little different; a sparkling hen fish, slender and elegant — or an up-jawed buck, stout and thick-girthed.

Lake Lenice epitomizes the desert fishing experience. It is located in a dramatic valley, east of the Columbia River and Highway 243 at the Crab Creek Wildlife Area. You see, there is no need to travel as far as New Zealand or even Montana. Extraordinary rainbows can be found here in most years. And looking past such minor annoyances as primitive campgrounds and a horizon framed in high-voltage power lines, the wildlife area itself is virtually pristine.

Several years ago, I made a quick trip across the Cascades with Ed Ruckey to sample spring fishing at Lenice and the adjacent Nunnally-Merry Lakes chain. This was an especially successful trip, worthy of mention if for no other reason than to pass on a few interesting observations and experiences. We arrived on a Thursday so that it would be easy to secure a camping spot in the sandy parking area near the trail into Lenice. The parking lot was almost empty. It was early May and perhaps, for a brief time, we would share the lake with no more than four or five other anglers. Perfect!

The sun was setting through a veil of drizzle. And although there is excellent trout action to be had at Lenice in the dark, we decided to postpone fishing until morning.

Later that night we were joined by Marc

Hurlbert and Errol McWhirk, friends from Bellingham. Errol has a well deserved reputation as a fine joke teller. He is one of those rare individuals who never forgets a funny story. However his repertoire includes 421 different "a sailor walks into a bar" jokes. Should you happen to meet him and not appreciate his sense of humor, do not disregard his acute knowledge of fly fishing — a gentler subject upon which he can expound for hours. After a few jokes and talk of the next day's anticipated insect hatches, we all turned in.

Next morning, I awoke to clear skies and the smell of a special Kansas City bacon Errol and Marc had bought in Ellensburg the day before. After a good breakfast, we all hit the west trail leading to Lenice. This is a preferred access point for the productive shallows and flats at the northwest end of the Lake. We thought about, but saw no rattlesnakes along the way.

Our float tube regatta entered the water and fanned out along the shoreline. For much of the day we drifted calmly, each picking up a fish or two every twenty minutes. Many were sleek, glimmering female rainbows of sixteen inches, decent fish exhibiting quick burst of speed on the initial run after the strike.

The trout were taking *chironomidae* below the surface. Chironomidae (AKA chironomids or midges) are an important part of a trout's diet in most Washington lakes. In fact, prior to the prolific appearance of the *callibaetis* mayfly, later in the month, the chironomid larvae or pupa imitation is the best fly pattern to cast at Lenice.

Chironomid larvae generally inhabit the lake bottom either in the mud or in an anchored, self-constructed tube. They appear as an elongated, inch worm shape with segmented body sections. Coloration varies from green or yellow to brown and black. Some mud dwelling species known as "blood worms" are red and actually contain hemoglobin. Northwest anglers obtain good results fishing an imitation of the larvae, near the bottom, which simulates the onset of the pupa stage of the insect's lifecycle.

The point in time at which the chironomid pupae wiggle to the lake's surface is of major significance to fly fishermen. During this slow, animated ascent the encased pupa is very susceptible to being eaten by trout. And many are. The ascent, if uninterrupted, lasts for several minutes.

When the pupa reaches the lake's surface, it sheds it's case or "shuck" (emerges) and completes metamorphosis to the adult. The winged adult, which looks like a small mosquito, is of less interest to the trout.

The first popular chironomid fly pattern in Washington was the "TDC", having been originated by Richard Thompson, a U.S. Fish and Wildlife Service biologist. TDC stands for Thompson's Delectable Chironomid, and it is appetizing, I suppose, if you are a trout.

In an early article, <u>Chironomids and Trout,</u> from the spring 1963 Washington Game Bulletin; Thompson describes the easy, original tie on a size 10 hook: (1) Tapered thread base over-wrapped with fine black chenille, (2) followed by five turns of silver tinsel rib, (3) finished with a collar of white ostrich herl (to mimic the feathery antennae found on more mature pupa) and topped by a head of dark thread.

There are now dozens of commercial chirono-mid patterns available, and many are simply a modification of the TDC. The old aphorism, *"imitation is the highest form of praise,"* surely applies. In another book I refer to the fly as "the venerable" TDC. Shortly after publication, Dick Thompson wrote to say that ... "just because it's 32 years old, doesn't really make it venerable. However, after looking up the meaning of the word ... calling forth respect through age, character, and attainments; I like it."

Well, any angler who has ever fished upon Washington still-waters with a fly rod likes it too sir, and we thank you!

Errol and I later moved into a small cove where we noticed what appeared to be large rainbows feeding against the grass. Their big fins were lightly rippling the water's surface. I approached with stealth.

After executing a straight backcast, I pushed the nine foot rod forward and placed my fly in a position that would precede the trout along it's perceived route. This is called "leading the fish", and it is a necessary tactic when sight fishing for "cruising" trout. I was still using a chironomid pupa, but the trout was not interested in what I had to offer.

Off to my right I recognized the problem, which would soon become the solution. Gray mayflies were beginning to emerge. A sign of the impending spring *callibaetis* mayfly hatches.

The bigger rainbows were being selective, preferring the mayfly to the midge. Before long I knotted-on a small gray soft hackle pattern and began looking for another active fish. And then I saw him.

The trout's caudal fin was waving back-and-forth; a fin at least as wide as my hand. He was casually slurping-up the emerging mayflies no more than twenty feet straight-away. I carefully dropped the fly in the path of his progress. The fly sat motionless just below the surface. As he turned and took it in, I held my breath and instinctively raised the rod high. The hook lodged firmly in a gristly jaw.

For just a moment both man and fish remained still. Suddenly, with a great surge of strength, the trout leaped forward. One, two, three, jumps and he was on the reel. It was a heavy fish, probably 23 or 24 inches in length and the jumps caused a tremendous commotion. Errol blurted out a somewhat irreverent but comforting word of encouragement. Then the five weight line went slack.

The fish had turned toward me and was still hooked. With the upper portion of his body now at the surface, the large trout shook, raised his head slowly — and methodically separated the leader close to the knot. That big rainbow had proved to be a challenging and memorable adversary.

However, as evening set-in, there would be new challenges. The chironomid emergence escalated once again, interspersed with swarms of caddis flies. The air was alive, and thick with winged adults.

Beneath the surface, our flashlights revealed a surrealistic plethora of illuminated insects. The lake was dead calm — almost eerie, and it was truly a great time to be fishing.

An impressionistic imitation of the emerging midge or caddis produced a sure strike every cast until it became completely dark.

On the hike back to camp that night the conversation shifted from monster rainbows to reptiles. The trail was poorly marked and uneven, so the idea of disturbing a rattlesnake made us all a little wary. A coyote howled and, for a while, everyone was quiet.

Errol, naturally, broke the silence . . . "a sailor walked into a bar."

The Dogs of Winter

The Nooksack is close to home. It is a river frozen in time because no dams impede it's flow. Although some small hydro-electric projects exist and more are proposed, the Nooksack's glacial melt remains interrupted only by a massive falls. The falls plunge dramatically over jagged rock almost fifty miles from the mouth, which is located at Lummi Reservation, south of Ferndale.

Above the falls, to it's source in the Cascades, lies a series of freshets, beaver ponds and spectacular montane habitat that is remote and lightly developed except for a few gold mines, logging operations and forest service roads leading to trailheads. Mt. Baker, an active volcano, sits high to the east. The old Mt. Baker Lodge and ski area were once the scene for film crew and cast of the famous Clark Gable movie, *Call of the Wild.*

Baker was a fitting place to record Jack London's classic tale of survival in the perilous snow country. The modern lift facility, now accessible by paved road, shuttles alpine skiers to some of the best powder and deepest base in western Washington.

When rural Whatcom County was settled in the 1880's, the lower Nooksack provided a convenient means of transportation for the pioneer farm communities of Lynden, Everson, and the local logging camps. The Lummi and Nooksack Tribes (the Coast or Straits Salish people) relied on the river as a primal point supplying the ecosystem so crucial to their coexistence with nature.

Great runs of salmon and steelhead navigated the river to spawn in it's tributaries laced from lowland meadows to canyon creeks. A report from the U.S. Fish Commissioner in 1897 provides data indicating that the yearly commercial catch of steelhead in the Nooksack may have exceeded 60,000 fish! Mere remnants of these early salmonid runs still prevail over new obstacles created from burdens placed upon the river by the demands of industrial developement.

The chum salmon (*Oncorhyncus Keta* - meaning "hooknose salmon") are interesting, often maligned fish. It seems that they have developed a reputation as the oily, less palatable salmon.

Chums can be good to eat if taken fresh from saltwater or before they have begun to deteriorate long in the river environment. In fact, the chum salmon may be beneficial to man in newly discovered ways. Nutritional research indicates that oily fish such as salmon, contain a unique class of fatty acids called Omega-3 (one of the few unsaturated fats found in foods of animal origin). Omega-3 has been shown to lower blood cholesterol levels, prevent blood clots, and thus reduce heart attack and stroke risk.

The primary reason chums are not well liked may stem from the lowly nickname, "dog salmon". Naturally, most people would be predisposed to reject the prospect of catching or, heaven forbid, eating anything called a "dog". The name "dog" especially applies to mature male specimens exhibiting large, canine-type teeth.

It could be that I am drawn to the chum salmon as a fisherman, because they receive less attention than the heralded king or coho. A rebellious, non-conformist attitude from my youth. More to the point, I find merit in chums because they are plentiful and, contrary to popular belief, very susceptible to being caught on a fly.

Chums are available to me in small Whatcom Creek, off Bellingham Bay at the Maritime Heritage Center, a few miles from my office. I have taken them here among a mass of shoulder to shoulder anglers and tangled lines. I can recall one lively (albeit foul-hooked) eighteen pounder leaping over and around this crowded affair, only to break off in one frantic dash toward Squalicum Harbor. Obviously, this fishing hole leaves much to be desired.

For solitude, a destination of choice is always the Nooksack, near Kendal; another half-hour drive. The chums can be found here as late as January, but fresh runs decline after Christmas. Our run in the Nooksack comes quite a bit later than that of the mighty Frazier drainage to the north in Canada.

The finest trip ever to this locale occurred during a lull in one of western Washington's worst storms, known as the Alaska Express. Cold air moving in from the Arctic can really rip-through this part of the state. However, at times during icy weather, the sun shines and the river is low and clear.

At two o'clock on a Saturday in December, Ed Ruckey and I drove up Highway 542 and parked about a mile from the spot we wanted to fish.

This was another of many, short trips we had made together since 1987.

Ed is a good fishing partner. He never complains about anything (although I complain to him) and he freely hands-out his expertly tied flies (so well arranged in fly boxes that they look like a set-up picture in some expensive catalog). Being an accomplished wildlife illustrator, quite knowledgeable on the subject of local animals and waterfowl, his observations in the field are always a welcome digression.

I pulled-in next to a white pickup truck where someone was leaning against the hood, busy assembling tackle. It was Lyle Hand, a respected elder of the Fourth Corner Fly Fishers and, acclaimed builder of split bamboo rods. He was about to test one of his two-piece creations. Lyle has a neat shop in town, where he makes limited quantities of these delicate wands for a very reasonable sum. With a little coaxing, he can also be persuaded to produce special form-bent trout nets from a variety of woods.

"That rod is much too nice for salmon fishing in weather like this," I called out. Somehow, we knew exactly what Lyle's reply would be.

"My rods are made to fish, not just to look at," was indeed the expected response. He went on to describe an innovative experimental design for the eight and one-half-foot rod's taper. Though Ed and I sincerely admired the finished product, neither of us quite understood the theory.

Our conversation soon ended as Lyle headed down river to proceed with his research. Ed was anxious to try a new section of water that had been carved-out by recent fall flooding, so I eagerly followed his lead. On the way, we crossed by a fast, deep slot that looked as if it might hold a dolly varden. The dolly varden trout (*Salvelinus malma*) is actually a char. They are, regretfully, becoming endangered in Puget Sound drainages and can now be subject to closed seasons in the region.

Several casts produced no dollies, but I managed to hook a large salmon that locked itself firmly into the current. My eight weight rod was inadequate for this situation and I could not budge the fish. To make matters more complicated, the drag on my old Hardy St. George reel was frozen, literally! I grabbed the running portion of the sink-tip line and broke the fish off at the leader, on purpose. Chums are, arguably, the strongest of salmon and can definitely wreck one's tackle; so I use a fairly light leader as a safety measure.

Ed had moved toward the calmer water that was our original quest. As I approached he was intently peering into a pool full of salmon. Mint bright fish swimming briskly and zig-zagging about. Prominent side-barring patterns and unblemished fins indicated that they had not taken long to arrive from the bay.

We took turns casting, and each retrieve produced a following of three or four chums. On almost every presentation a fish was hooked, played and successfully released. All were ten pounds or better, and full of fight.

The dogs really attacked the fly that day. Curiously, salmon do not feed once they enter the river in spawning sequence; they do however possess instincts or imprinted behavior from life at sea, which must cause them to bite at the imitation.

A fluorescent lime-green baitfish pattern, designed by northwest fly tyer Marc Hurlbert, is a most appealing chum salmon fly. It is aptly named "Dog Chow" and has become kind of famous around here due to the mention of it in a national fishing magazine. To be truthful, however, there is no secret formula or mystery in fly selection for chums; although a greenish body and some flashy material in the wing make a superior combination.

We continued fishing until our arms became weary and hands ached from the bitter chill. It was getting late and I could barely see the assembly of bald eagles atop alder snags that lined the ridge above. Adult eagles were scavenging liberally on the decaying salmon carcasses.

These majestic raptors winter at the Nooksack because the salmon are here. Should the salmon ever disappear — so too would the eagles. Further; the spent salmon, as they decompose, replenish critical nutrients on the river bottom for inhabiting organisms. This is the fish's final act following a reproductive performance that is vital to both man and beast.

The eagles swooped down from their high perch, landing at the exposed edge of the gravel bar next to the water. But they were nervous, alarmed by our presence.

Content to have shared a few Nooksack salmon with them, we left treading softly. And I felt like an intruder, as it grew dark.

Chopaka

In a high valley, due north of Toats Coulee and west of the small town of Loomis, lies a jewel of a lake called Chopaka.

Chopaka has long been a choice destination for Washington fly fishers who undertake a pilgrimage each spring to fish the famous *callibaetis* mayfly hatch. This particular insect emergence has become so popular over the years that some local anglers simply refer to the callibaetis as the "Chopaka may".

Most Seattlites make their way to Chopaka via the east-bound lanes of highways 90 or 20. Those of us living in the northwest corner of the state, save about an hours driving time traveling through Canada.

Canada Highway 3 passes through Manning Provincial Park and the rich Similkameen River drainage. The route returns to the U.S. by dropping down into the border crossing at Nighthawk

— a desolate, dusty corner of Okanogan County. In fact, the quaint border patrol station is open only limited hours, so a late arrival will necessitate a long detour to Osoyos.

After skirting the edge of huge Palmer Lake, an impoundment known for it's excellent bass fishing — some nail-biting begins. The final steep ascent to Chopaka can be quite hair-raising in a good spring rain. Four wheel drive vehicles afford the best opportunity for a safe journey at that time of the year. In the fall, I have crawled up the intimidating grade with my old station wagon, albeit still for want of traction in the loose spots.

Attaining the perfectly carved niche wherein the lake sits, the dirt and gravel road runs over an expansive cattle ranch surrounded by magnificent hills dotted with conifers. On a windy day, the lake itself may be indistinguishable from the shoreline. Choppy water blends well into the tall, bowing sedge grasses.

Fishing Chopaka, mid-week, reminds us that we can still find lakes in the Pacific Northwest where the trout are eager — and anglers are few. Conversely, visiting Chopaka on a prime spring weekend reinforces the thought that "things ain't what they used to be."

Sometimes, the lake and camp areas are virtually abandoned, making for an idealic number of maybe a dozen anglers on the water. It was to such a setting that Dick Van Demark and I arrived last season.

What we found, along with the sparse population of fly fishers, was a tremendous lack of visible insect activity. We were, however, undaunted by the less-than-perfect looking conditions, and proceeded to raise the tent.

Fair weather in Okanogan County during late fall is a hit or miss proposition. As luck would have it, we were treated to clear skies at dawn. I noticed that several fishermen were up early, casting a floating line and the typical "Adams style" dry fly (always a fair likeness to the slender gray callibaetis adult). Nevertheless, little action was to be had, probably due to the fact that the number of mayflies showing on the water at that time of the year was not significant enough to motivate big trout. I would guess the lake's traditional reputation as dry fly water sticks in an angler's mind, regardless of what reality might dictate.

We were there to catch and photograph some impressive rainbows, so Dick and I began to observe and experiment.

My friend, Dick Van Demark, is without question the best fly fisherman I have ever seen. For a good many years he has been a patient angling *sensei*, whose tutelage has served me well.

In the forward to Dick's book, <u>Steelhead Fly Fishing in Low Water - *a different approach*</u>, Bob Barnes propounds "... he (Dick) challenges himself and his companions to discard the trappings of the pedantic and to probe ever deeper into the mores of the sport of angling and to explore our understanding of why fish do what they do. He is a restless and inquisitive spirit." Well said.

It is also true that Dick possesses a unique combination of physical angling skills, on-water experience, and scientific knowledge that enable him to analyze most trout fishing situations and quickly meet with success. Further, he can consistently make known practical solutions to what seem to be unsolvable aquatic mysteries.

Though this day at Chopaka no astounding angling revelations were forthcoming. He simply reached into the shallows, pulled-out some vegetation by the roots and identified a hand-full of green shrimp (scuds) clinging thereto.

I secured a #10 Green Marabou Nymph to my medium sinking line. These attractor flies are conceived with an all-marabou body for lifelike movement superior to the compacted bodies made by dubbing such coarse materials as wool or hare's mask.

To our delight, the mature Chopaka rainbows were attracted to these nymphs. Each short cast and slow drift produced a nibble akin to trout taking a stationary bait. The medium sink-rate line helped maneuver the fly just above the bottom vegetation and mosses, thus no snags.

I could see the trout as they methodically approached and struck from below, producing a rhythmic "thump, thump, thump" from the fly rod tip. More often than not, a hook-up ensued. Once engaged, the healthy eighteen to twenty-two inch fish were off and jumping — frequently running into the backing on my lightweight reel.

We took turns focusing the camera on each other until both our enthusiasm and the roll of film had been exhausted.

Then, a most unusual occurrence drew our attention to a small cove. Adult dragonflies were buzzing and zipping around in apparent reproductive habit. Predator trout were leaping head-and-tail into the air, in an attempt to inhale the mating dragon pairs. Before long, another fly fisherman came upon the scene and began furiously casting a massive dry fly in a vain attempt to "match the hatch". Maybe his presentation should have included two large flies tied together. I don't know. I paddled away thinking he at least had the perseverance to keep trying despite the odds.

*   *   *   *   *

As a side note to those hardy souls not satisfied with an entire day on the water: Plenty of folks fish all night at Chopaka. I personally find night fishing in a float tube to be wet, cold, and tiring. However, fishing the midnight hour with a leech pattern can be very productive, so the temptation to go out is always there. The biggest fish are hooked in the dark, or they at least feel like the biggest fish — my night vision is so terrible that I can't see a damn thing no matter how bright my flashlight is.

I once became disoriented while night fishing at Chopaka in a float tube. I drifted for fifteen minutes before I could figure out where I was. I can recall feeling like a kid alone in a dark alley, taking out the trash. I wanted to run back into a warm, safe house.

The wind whistled upon the water's surface. What must have been a muskrat created strange movement near shore. Cows on the far bank groaned a low chant and the sound of away-off thunder fell into the valley. An ancient angling poem then crossed my mind. I could remember the last two chilling lines "... Percephone fulfill my wish — that my ghost shall catch the ghosts of fish."

I believe that if a fish had pulled on my line at that moment, I would have jumped clear out of my waders and joined that mythical goddess of the underworld along with most all the fine angling brethren of the past.

I was sort of relieved when out of nowhere Van Demark approached and said: "you look a little lost, Danny."

Night fishing is indeed a cool adventure. Don't forget to bring warm clothes, extra leader, and your best imagination.

Smallmouth

"Inch for inch, and pound for pound, the gamest fish that swims." These are the immortal words of Dr. James Henshall, author of the spiny ray classic, <u>Book of the Black Bass</u> (revised edition 1904). He was not, those many years ago, describing the ever popular largemouth bass — prize quarry to millions of devoted bait casters from Florida to California. Henshall boldly pegs the smallmouth black bass as the better fighter of the two, and goes a step further in placing the smallmouth ahead of our beloved trout in terms of spunk.

Now, Henshall may be out of line and overly theatrical, so I question his accuracy. And, probably, if a smallmouth were enlarged to the size of an albacore, the long-finned tuna might not have met it's match. Regardless of any comparisons, it is a known fact that the smallmouth bass is a worthy adversary on a fly rod.

Fly fishing for smallmouth (AKA *bronze backs* or *red eyes*) is a challenging alternative for the trout angler looking to expand his or her fly fishing horizons. Moreover, it is conceivable that the smallmouth and other spiny ray species will have elevated significance in the future of fresh water sport fishing across the northwest region, especially in Washington State.

As our population explodes, urban lakes will be more heavily subjected to man's influence, forming habitat less likely to support trout or other salmonids. Twenty years from now, will the last weekend in April be "opening day of the bass season"? I doubt it. However, contingents of die-hard bass anglers in Olympia are already advocating the development of better warm water species lakes capable of yielding larger bass. With regulations properly enforced, this type of fishing could be very interesting. Unlike most stocked trout, the bass would maintain better longevity and reproductive abilities. And what about fly-fishing-only bass lakes. The tournament gang wouldn't appreciate this idea, but it sounds good to me.

The smallmouth bass is certainly not native to Washington or the pacific coast. It's native range lies from Minnesota down to Georgia and only as far west as Oklahoma. In 1874, Deputy U.S. Fish Commissioner Livingston Stone transported a load of smallmouth two thousand miles west by rail to California, in an aquarium car. This is documented as the first introduction of the species in the Pacific region.

According to Ben Hur Lampman, in his little know treasure <u>The Coming of the Pond Fishes</u> (1946), the first smallmouth to enter Washington state were not introduced by any government agency. It is thought that at some time prior to 1924, members of a logging company working on Blakely Island stocked a lake there with Michigan smallmouth. Subsequently, an Oregon Game Warden removed some of these bass to his state in order to establish a Willamette River fishery. The possibility then exists that the offspring of the original Blakely Island bass, or a later generation, made their way into the Columbia system (and consequently the Yakima and Snake Rivers). The Columbia River smallmouth population is today one of the more productive in the country. Those Blakely Island via Michigan bass have sure come a long way!

The actual practice of fly fishing for bass, in America, pretty much began when eastern trout anglers came upon the fish by accident. The earliest recorded fly fishing catch that I have found is listed in Genio Scott's <u>Fishing in American Waters</u> (1875). Scott relates just a small footnote regarding "northern bass"(smallmouth) taken on the artificial fly by a party of anglers in 1837. Another report mentions a Scottish tourist to the east coast who landed several "largemouth salmon" on trout flies during the summer of 1850 (<u>American Angler's Book</u>, T. Norris, 1864).

Evidence indicates that many early fly caught bass were juveniles, since anglers used small top water flies or wet flies designed for brook trout. Apparently, outdoor writers of the time disseminated certain stereotypes or rigid theories about fly fishing and bass. To quote Henshall:

". . . it is a truism that the largest fish (bass) do not, as a rule, take the artificial fly. Those who wish to lure the finny giants must perforce use bait or the trolling spoon."

Henshall's theory can be looked upon as legitimate with respect to the flies available at the time. I suppose it never occurred to him that an artificial fly might be constructed to imitate food forms attractive to big, mature bass.

Early twentieth century tackle houses did carry

a variety of special bass flies. In <u>Professional Fly Tying and Tackle Making</u> (1941), George Herter describes the steps to creating bass fly "wings". His bass flies were very similar to an eastern trout wet fly with the wing fashioned from a round duck flank feather. Again, it is clear that American fly fishers were still convinced that bass flies should resemble mayflies, albeit bigger mayflies.

There were, of course, a few fly rod "lures" on the market called bass bugs or feather minnows. Light lures like Heddon's *Wilderdilg* and the earlier hand made *Devil Bugs* can be traced back to 1911. A reference in <u>Field Book of Fresh Water Angling</u> (J.A. Knight, 1944) alludes to even earlier, pre-1900, cork and feather fly rod lures called *Spatters*. But it was not until the 1970s that innovative fly fishermen such as Dave Whitlock pioneered the design and use of larger, sub-surface bass flies.

Tied-on-the-vise sculpin, minnows, frogs, and mice are now regularly fished for big bass with great success. My favorite sub-surface smallmouth pattern is a moose mane crayfish presented on a full sinking line along lake shores and below boat docks or tree cover. Smallmouth are very aggressive feeders and will take a large streamer or zonker as well. They are the only fresh water fish I have ever seen swim off their spawning bed to attack an angler. On several occasions, while float tubing a shallow lake, my fins have been bitten by pugnacious bass.

There are a variety of Washington destinations where smallmouth are found: The aforementioned Columbia, Snake, and Yakima Rivers; Banks, Potholes, and Moses Lakes in Grant County; Palmer Lake in Okanogan County; Mayfield Lake in Lewis County; or Seattle area Lakes Washington and Sammamish to name a few.

I consider myself lucky because excellent bass water can be seen from the family room of my home. Nevertheless, whenever I think of smallmouth bass, I think of a more distant location and the five pounder that was to be the only fish I hooked that day. The curious part of this story is not the heavy bass nor the struggle to land it. What I came away with from the event was a rare discovery. I was able to affirm something I had always suspected about the quasi-mystical side of bass fishing.

Funny thing; I knew beforehand that the big bass was going to strike. I'm not exactly sure how I knew, but I think it must have been "the touch". I have never been able to explain precisely what "the touch" is, except to say that it exists and I have always had it. Perhaps it is a gut feeling, a primitive knowledge or instinct that tells me the technique I am using will work or where I am casting is correct.

Most all dedicated anglers have "the touch" and take it for granted. It may be an acquired skill or it may be deep rooted, genetic and profound. On the other hand, as my wife interjects, it may be that I am full of baloney. She insists that fishing should not be elevated to the level of religion — it's just a sport. God did not infuse some of us with special fishing instincts and leave others to sit woefully inept at water's edge.

For the sake of debate, let it be known that the late Lummi Carver, Gary Hillaire, once told me how certain people of the northwest native cultures have specific, designated tribal duties which are divinely guided. Who could argue with that! I would claim fishing is one of these duties and the person responsible for this task would surely have "the touch" plus a portion of angling knowledge passed-down from an elder or two.

Decide for yourself if "the touch" is real, if you have it, or if you care to have it — because I have said enough. Remember, I am full of baloney.

And as my friend Gary (Seahtlhuk) might have advised; "Don't talk the walk, walk the talk" or "be silent and fish well."

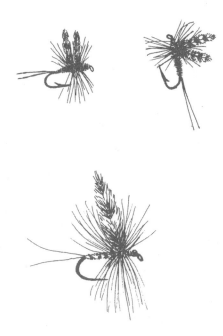

The Poacher

The following story is loosely based on a true incident that took place not so long ago on one of Washington's most esteemed rivers. It serves to illustrate a silly conflict over choice of methods in the fishing world — creating a wall of jealousy and misunderstanding which separates the purist fly fisherman from the traditional bait caster. An aggravating rift that has existed for decades in America. Oh, at least we Yanks aren't so picky as the English — who carry on in discord over the nymph versus dry fly controversy (a sharp division within the fly fishing ranks, alone!).

Now on with the story, where I have altered the setting, combined several characters and changed names so as not to offend a soul.

Paul was a personality in transition. For the twelve years we had been acquainted, he had proved to be a trusted yet pig-headed friend.

Every cause in which he believed became a quest to vanquish the opposition. In his endeavors, he always seemed to focus on hostility rather than try to accomplish any good. He took very seriously, his role of radical environmentalist and self-proclaimed protector of mankind.

In desperation, on occasion, Paul had entered into physical altercation with opponents; his least revered adversary being "those beer swilling hicks" known as bait fishermen. My buddy was bad to the bone.

But I had seen a change come over Paul in recent months and became impressed with his ability to defuse lifelong habits of anger and suspicion. I know from experience that behavioral traits are hard to modify and it is a fortunate individual who has enough integrity to take action and bring about results. Now a genuine kindness and goodwill radiated from the man most of the time. However, Paul's greatest challenge was at hand. And it materialized during a trout fishing trip, with me of course.

After a good day on the river, we clamored out of the current and over the silt to begin a slow walk back to town. A sign at waterside read . . .

FLY FISHING ONLY

SINGLE BARBLESS HOOKS
CATCH AND *FILLET*

Some idiot, probably a pimply faced adolescent, had crossed out the word *RELEASE* and scrawled over it his own ideology. Paul had steam blowing out of his ears.

Moving along three hundred yards, we came to the Dead Tree Riffle; best dry fly water the stream had to offer — a long cedar shaded run with plenty of rainbows stacked beneath some rotting trees.

A burly figure was standing on the opposite bank. He was close to six-seven and fat, but strong like a wrestler on late night TV.

The "Wrestler" was bending over a rusty can of live, red wigglers and upon approach from behind we could see a distinct posterior cleavage rising high above the elastic waistband of his white BVD's.

Paul bristled like a grizzly protecting it's cache. Hell, this was the enemy invading the Dead Tree Riffle. A stereotypical bait fisher in the flesh. I started thinking that perhaps Paul hadn't changed much — this was like old times and I could predict a fight was about to ensue. Two dead fish in the bushes didn't help matters either.

When we confronted the Giant, he turned quickly and greeted us with a slow drawl of a burp — he was clutching an empty bottle of Bud and working on a chaw. My God, the stereotype exacerbated. This was real trouble!

Paul looked him straight in the eye and the big stranger spit, missing my foot by an inch with the partially masticated quid. That made <u>me</u> mad.

I imagined a terrifying battle wherein Paul got trounced and yours truly was left to defend his honor. Guess I could always outrun the blubbery foe, leaving him breathless and incapacitated.

I returned from the fantasy to discover that the hulky bait chucker had moved closer and was <u>smiling</u>. Not a phony smirk, but a wide, yellow toothy sort of grin. To our surprise he was equipped with a fly rod — probably a fake outfit just in case some fellers like us showed up. His spin-casting rig was certainly stowed in the brush next to the two gutted trout.

"Hullo boys", he said in a friendly voice. "I been fishin here all day en jest caught them two little trout there - not hardly worth cookin."

"Not hardly worth cookin!" Well at that Paul was about to attack with his fists, but held back for some reason and proceeded with a verbal assault instead.

"Didn't you read the regulations, man . . . this is catch and release water — fly fishing only, pal!"

"Ahm real sorry boys", the stranger replied sheepishly. "I was usin this fly pole to flip them nightcrawlers over by that stump. Nobody ever taught me how ta fish with real flies. Ah would if ah could. Suppose ah'l haf ta stop fishin now, huh?"

Paul's attitude toward the man changed in an instant. He could recognize a decent human when he saw one and, besides, the stranger acted sincere — a poacher no more.

The confrontation subsided. Paul spent the remaining hours of light teaching his new friend how to cast a fly. The stranger, who's name turned out to be Bubba (just kidding) was even kind enough to share some chips with us. No doubt he had saved them for an accompaniment to his trout dinner. Shucks, given enough fritos and bean dip, I'm sure the guy would have gratuitously shown Paul how to Texas-rig a plastic worm.

However, the food ran out. So don't expect to see Paul on "Bassmasters" any time soon. He's still a purist fly fisherman, and he still has a bad attitude once in a while. But he is moving in the right direction and that's what counts.

I learned something that day. Maybe the stranger was a flagrant liar and the lowest dog ever to tote a fly rod. But maybe, just maybe he realized us fly dudes weren't so bad after all. What the heck, he might obey the law next time, or at least I like to think so.

And if the truth be known, before he became an elitist snob, Paul himself used to crank a bait or soak a rind now and then. So who's foolin who.

There's a little of Paul . . . and Bubba in all of us!

Nostalgia

T he first fishing book I ever read was Arnold Gingrich's *Well Tempered Angler.* I recall how my Dad pulled it from his bulky suitcase, after returning from one of many business trips that year. Upon presenting it to me, he affectionately grumbled something about "not understanding why I fished." And though my father really disliked fishing, we both shared a deep appreciation for books, so the gift was well chosen.

A brief chapter in the book centered on the subject of premium fly tackle, particularly bamboo fly rods and English trout reels. Although Gingrich was pre-occupied with diminutive midge rods and traditional east coast equipment, his engaging style had an affect on me. I, like countless other anglers, soon realized an admiration for the fine and hand made.

Fly fishers are, indeed, tackle nuts. Most own

a bundle of rods with at least three or four reels, extra spools, and every conceivable form of line configuration, gadget and device. And more flies than could be cast in one thousand years. While new tackle, fresh from the maker's factory, holds some degree of excitement for the majority of consumers — it is tackle from the past that can bring about a serious emotional response from the avid angler.

Why do people collect old fishing tackle? Why do we covet any thing ancient and antique? I contend that it must be *nostalgia* — clearly a yearning for what is perceived to have been a gentler and simpler time, and probably was. Here lies the heart of the matter. We miss what is past, not necessarily the era in history but our own childhood. A time when we knew not much and worried little.

Of all things angling, the bamboo rod most strongly represents the past. It is true that these lilting instruments of the lake and stream are still built by hand. A few stalwart craftsmen can yet be found splitting bamboo culms (tonkin cane) and hand-beveling the thin individual strips, which are glued-up to form a hexagonal blank. When fully adorned and finished the great rod, contemporary though it may be, is worthy of a king's ransom.

Old, used bamboo rods are different. Each one seems to have a story to tell — of fish and perhaps a little about the angler who's palm encircled the soiled cork grip. Occasionally, the story is known, but usually it is not. New owners, in turn, contribute their own part to the ongoing heritage.

Being a collector myself, I have owned many nice bamboo fly rods. Leonard, Paine, Granger, Heddon, Phillipson, and even a Montaque or two. Recently, while contemplating a growing family and feeling guilty about a closet-full of valuable gear, I sold most of my bamboo sticks. I remember some rods, not in a bizarre spiritual way, just fondly. The "Winston" rod is one of these.

About ten years ago, it was my pleasure to receive an especially beautiful classic bamboo rod with an interesting history. Being a resident of the Pacific Northwest, I was logically drawn toward long rods suited to fishing in a brisk wind or on open, fast water. This rod was long and light, a combination of attributes not always associated with cane.

By correspondence with a dealer in Georgia, I was able to purchase the early, Stoner built Winston tucked in the original bag and labeled aluminum tube. It arrived encumbered with a bit of disrepair, having rusted guides and a loose ferrule. However, at nine feet and exhibiting a delicate tip, it might cast a seven weight line with great ease. The old varnish smelled like forty seasons of opening days. And the price was right!

The rod was first owned by the late author Henry Bruns, who wrote me a letter after learning it had come into my possession. Evidently, Hank had used the rod for "research" while gathering information about trout fishing in Northern California, Oregon, and Washington. His assignment was to draft a travel article for *Sunset Magazine* and the rod was found to be ideal for subduing big resident rainbows, coastal cutthroat and steelhead along the way. In fact, he procured the rod directly from the legendary Lew Stoner at his San Francisco shop. Although Stoner was apparently hard of hearing, Bruns was able to communicate his needs well enough. By the tone of his letter to me, I learned of his affection for this rod.

I liked the rod too, but was afraid to actually fish it, since the rough guides would tear-up a good fly line and the loose male ferrule would surely damage the bamboo itself. For five years I procrastinated about having it professionally refinished, hesitant to alter the original character and patina. Finally, as Mr. Bruns himself had done, I parted with it. I traded the Winston to a well known attorney in Anacortes, because he had just "the rod" I was looking for — an Orvis Limestone Special of eight and one half feet in mint condition, ready to fish.

Months later I got a call from Dwight Lyons, a friend and expert rod restorer in Portland. The Winston had been sent to Dwight who had somehow found a spool of old guide wrapping silk that was an exact match. He then refinished the rod to original specifications.

Dwight's words still ring in my ear: "Dan, why didn't you keep that rod!" I should have.

Survivors of the Stone Wind

From an early age I was fascinated by science fiction. Being especially attracted to film; I grew-up watching movies like *The Time Machine*, *Planet of the Apes*, and *Journey to the Center of the Earth*.

At the core, if you will, of these not-so-epic but palatable stories was always a volcanic explosion, violent earthquake, social upheaval, or environmental catastrophe. Often these portentous events were followed by the regeneration of nature.

On May 18, 1980; Washington's youngest volcano erupted. The event of Mount St. Helens was an opportunity for us all to observe real life, natural drama. Science non-fiction! For this was an earthy conflagration — not of man, his weapons or machines. A true, organic definition of the legal term "act of God".

The most amazing part of the St. Helens story, aside from the personal acts of courage displayed by residents of the area, is the subsequent regeneration of plant and animal populations in the blast zone. To fully appreciate how these organisms survived to thrive again, one must first consider the devastation that took place.

As the north rim of Mt. St. Helens collapsed, super-heated, pressurized water trapped inside the volcano was suddenly released. Expanding steam and hot gasses exploded out the side. This lateral blast fragmented the mountain side forming a **stone-filled wind** that hugged the ground, traveling at speeds in excess of 600 miles per hour. Large fragments of the former summit were to follow in an avalanche of heavy rock and debris.

Animals in the immediate blast zone escaped only if they were underground. Some plant roots further from the volcano were spared if sheltered by stumps or boulders.

Fortunately, at the higher elevations in mid-May, lakes were still covered with a thick layer of ice, so trout were shielded from the eruption. Other fish and amphibians in nearby streams were not so lucky, and perished — suffocated in ash-choked waters.

Those surviving brook and cutthroat trout in the alpine lakes have now colonized other waters by migrating down small outlet streams and forming new populations.

Land animals and vegetation have been equally resilient. As the stone wind pulverized trees in its path; needles and branches were carried away and deposited as a layer of organic debris or compost. This material became a source of nutrients for returning plant life. Small rodents, ascending to the surface from deep burrows, provided a fertile foothold for the recovering ecosystem by contributing nutrient rich feces to the top soil. This initial surviving population of pocket gophers and mice died-out after three years due to a lack of food, however their remains continued to fertilize the soil. As plants grew, the Toutle elk herd returned to graze in traditional habitat and other animals gradually migrated in or spread out from nearby areas.

Man has contributed to the reforestation and aided the recovery through protective regulations which encourage natural renewal. Some select aquatic habitats, including famous Spirit Lake, are set aside for scientific study.

Spirit Lake remains a restricted area for good

reason. Biologists want to observe the natural progress of the post-volcanic environment there. Other waters are open to public visitation and light impact recreation. Coldwater lake falls into this category. And so it is of great interest to the fly fisher.

Seven hundred acre Coldwater Lake was created by an avalanche of volcanic fragments that inundated and clogged Coldwater Creek at the base of the mountain. The rock and ash created a dam that was considered to be unstable and subject to erosion. To minimize flood danger in the area below the new lake, the U.S. Army Corp. of Engineers reinforced and stabilized the natural dam.

Then, in 1989, the decision was made to plant 30,000 rainbow trout in Coldwater — and the fish were introduced as fry that year. The rainbows developed and have reproduced on their own, sustaining a fair size population since the lake opened to good fishing in 1993. With the help of strict *Selective Fishery Regulations*, the lake will continue to provide a unique destination with potential for the experienced fly caster skilled in the art of delicate presentation.

A canoe or float tube is an adequate craft upon which to propel along the barren shoreline and predominant shallows. Internal combustion engines are not allowed, and boaters are asked to stay afloat. Trampling the fragile ground is not an act favored by the Forest Service staff, so stay in designated areas only.

In addition to the cruising 14 to 20 inch rainbows that inhabit Coldwater, a few cutthroat trout are found here, having swam from higher elevations after surviving the eruption.

Another destination, Castle Lake, sits within full view of the Visitor Center, tucked into a jagged crag, looking much like a set for *Jurrasic Park*. The vicinity of the lake can be reached via logging roads, but access to the water requires a risky, steep ascent down the southwest bank. For the adventurous angler or, better yet, rock climber — Castle may hold a thirty inch trout. A miracle fish. . . A survivor of the stone wind!

The Quiet Pool

Somewhere, on the Washington and British Columbia border, flows a headwater stream. Classic, blue ribbon trout water under the shroud of a glacial peak — gateway to one of the most remote and untraveled wilderness areas of the United States. An area not for the faint of heart; not easily attainable except by an axle-crunching, rough road or by switchback trail.

If you have ever coveted a secret fishing spot, then understand why I choose to withhold the exact location of this stream. Quite a few others consider this spectacular free stone water to be their "secret" too. Perhaps you are among those privy to it's coordinates, or you may be able to deduce it's whereabouts from this writing. Under the circumstances, I can only share my feelings for the place and someday, maybe, you will find it, appreciate it and help to protect it.

Resident trout rivers are rare in the Northwest. We have, of course, great rivers. But most twist and snake east to west until they commingle with salt water in the sounds, bays and straits off the coast. The predominant inhabiting trout are not resident but anadramous species, and include the famed sea going rainbow known as steelhead.

In contrast, "my river" holds resident rainbow trout. Yet they display characteristics similar to migratory fish. The difference is that these trout do not migrate to salt water — but to an azure lake down stream. Biologists theorize that the fish may be lineal descendants of native steelhead, thought to have been trapped when the lake was formed by construction of a barrier dam prior to World War Two.

What we have then is a light-tackle angler's dream. A strain of miniature steelhead that emulate their sea-run relatives by utilizing the lake in the same way true steelhead out-migrate to the ocean. Well not quite the same way, since these rainbows feed more heavily in the tributary streams branching out from the lake rather than in the lake itself. And that is precisely why fly fishing for them is so productive.

After spawning in early summer, the fish gain strength dining on a sumptuous in-stream repast of aquatic and terrestrial insects.

By August, when the stream clears and lowers, fishing is in full swing. An assortment of challenging hatches can be imitated by the accomplished angler; including small yellow stonefly nymphs, fast water caddis larvae and for the dry fly fisher, a superb evening *baetis* emergence.

The main feature is the activity of a large mayfly nymph known as green drake. In mid-August, the rainbows become very aggressive to the nymph in the morning and again to the winged adult in the afternoon.

The sheer number of "bugs" available here is thrilling. In fact, on a trip to the area during the summer of 1988, entomologist Rick Hafele described the river as one with a truly unique variety of aquatic insects. I still have the samples he helped me collect a short distance from our gravel bar camp.

Yes, this is premium trout water and more. It was revealed to me by a generous friend many years ago. A gift not forgotten.

I submit that trout water such as this breeds contempt. Contempt for a plastic, decadent, and dangerous world not far away. The sounds and smells are different here, and a few days on-stream are much needed to cleanse the senses of populated squalor and frenzied work weeks.

A calm respite of angling, looking, and listening can soothe that contempt. It reminds us that there is still peace and solitude outside the tumult of a material society and self.

Poets and outdoor writers have long addressed the query: "Why do we fish."

The late Roderick Haig-Brown, the one upon whom many northwest anglers rely for inspirational fishing prose, once wrote that he did not know why he fished or why other men fished. But he then went on to explain exactly why! And it is logically so. "We like it and it makes us think and feel".

Fishing provides us with an opportunity to escape from everyday routine and transform our thoughts into what should be a relaxed, enjoyable pursuit.

It has been said that the pure act of angling should be approached with no clear goal, no set agenda, and no sense of time. However this euphoric state of mind may be unrealistic and potentially boring. Most of us certainly don't want to meditate and fall upon the water between every cast. The average angler welcomes and accepts the challenge of the pursuit. This is part of the game.

The sport of fishing, especially fly fishing, is a blend of uncountable, fascinating techniques and practices to hold one's interest. Anglers find pleasure in these methods and tactics, and for many, they become a major attraction to the sport.

At the extreme, we find some fisher people who become so serious about the pursuit, so out of balance, and so fully dedicated to success, that they achieve no renewal of spirit nor even a scintilla of recreation. This is sad.

I am reminded of all these things when I enter a favorite section of my stream. It is called the quiet pool.

For what reasons do I fish? I can say that in a lifetime of angling I have personally touched upon all reasons, fallen into all categories and, at times, have needed an attitude adjustment or two. But here, at the quiet pool, it is possible to achieve the consummate outdoor experience. Where smells bring about only good memories; where one could be content with wind blown maple leaves instead of mayflies, and submerged rocks could suffice as trout — it would not matter. For this is the greater bounty.

I think this is really what we are after, and this is why we fish.

Island Lakes

W hen Washington fishermen talk of the San Juan Islands, the conversation usually involves salmon, saltwater, downriggers, and marine weather.

People from out of the region might even think the San Juans are located somewhere near Puerto Rico and wonder how all those salmon live so close to the equator.

Four islands, in particular, provide an added fishing bonus for anyone venturing ashore with a fly rod. Lopez, Orcas, San Juan, and Fidalgo all possess sizable fresh water lakes as a part of their inland geography.

The San Juan archipelago encompasses approximately 200 named islands, in addition to a multitude of protrusions, exposed rocks, and shelves. All within a few miles of the Washington State Ferry Terminal at Anacortes.

For many years the natural harbors of the San

Juans have been recognized as prime moorage or calm anchorage for yachters voyaging north to British Columbia's Gulf Islands, The Queen Charlottes, or Southeast Alaska. Until the 1980's, the roads, trails, and parks in all but the biggest towns (Friday Harbor and Eastsound), had basically remained "undiscovered" except by Puget Sound locals. Now, like everywhere else that was any good to visit, real estate speculation and tourist traffic have caused the main islands to become congested during the warm summer months.

My kids still love the San Juans. So we go as often as possible. The highlight of any family trip to the outer islands is the journey across Rosario Straight. Our beloved ferry, "The Nisqually", offers a smooth sail, great coffee, decent food, and most of all, a pleasing brass and wood nautical decor. The prospect of sighting a pod of whales always adds to the excitement.

I find the very best time to fish the wonderful island lakes is at mid-week, just before or just after the main tourist season. Opening day trout fishing is likely good at Cascade Lake within the borders of Moran State Park on Orcas Island. Veteran fly fishers are well aware of the nice rainbows that can be found there in May and June.

Close-by, at the base of Mt. Constitution, is enchanting Mountain Lake, the largest body of fresh water in the County. Kokanee (landlocked sockeye salmon) are a best bet here and usually plentiful. Internal combustion engines are not allowed on the lake, so it is an ideal place to row, paddle, or hike — offering more solitude than Cascade, on a crowded weekend.

If you have the ability to trailer a small boat over to Orcas, a unique opportunity exists. After sampling the action at one of the aforementioned lakes, a short drive to snug Deer Harbor can lead to some saltwater salmon or bottom fishing. The neat thing about this area is it's sheltered proximity to endless submerged reefs and drop-offs capable of yielding excellent results. A sturdy craft can be beached at nearby Fawn Island for a picnic — or run two miles west to Jones Island State Park for a bigger adventure.

On Fidalgo Island, closer to the mainland, sits one of the best fly fishing lakes in Washington. Of course, Fidalgo is only an island by virtue of it's position to the west of the Swinomish Channel in Skagit County. And it is very accessible via a major highway bridge. Nevertheless, only a stones throw from the throng of vacationers in Deception Pass State Park is famous Pass

Lake.

Pass has been a fly-fishing-only lake since 1942, one of the first in the country to receive this special regulation status. At that time, it was a cutthroat lake producing many fish in the ten to sixteen inch range.

During the last ten years, biologists have attempted to establish an atlantic salmon fishery at Pass similar to that of Hosmer Lake in Central Oregon. After a fling with these landlocked atlantics, the lake has now settled into it's current reputation as a solid producer of large rainbow trout year after year.

The lake is monitored by the Fidalgo Fly Fishers, a conservation minded club based in Skagit County. Anglers are asked to record their success, or lack thereof, on a ledger located at a small shelter near the boat launch. I have taken rainbows up to nineteen inches at Pass, but they get much bigger according to the data collected.

Most popular of the wet or sub-surface fly patterns at Pass is the chironomid imitation. Early spring is a favorite time for anglers to suspend a weighted red chironomid (blood worm) off the bottom on a long leader and floating line. Pass regulars affix a small "corkie" to the butt section of the leader with a piece of toothpick. This rig acts as a strike indicator and depth adjuster. Brown and black versions of the pattern will also serve well to imitate the small larva as they escape their muddy fortress and begin wiggling toward the lake surface.

On one pleasant April trip to Pass in 1990, I was accompanied by Peter Mills, an ardent angler who swore by a fly he called the "Psychedelic Blue Chironomid". And it was truly florescent blue — almost hurt your eyes to look at it. However, it caught fish (as a matter of fact several very healthy rainbows that day). I figured the fish must have seen another color reflected in the blue tinsel body of the brilliant, yet unconventional fly. As I look back on the day, I remember we had been eating cold-smoked salmon, which was quite odoriferous. Maybe the salmon scent from our hands got on the funny blue flies and attracted those trout. There had to be some logical explanation!

The best strategy for fly selection at Pass can be gleaned from the writings of legendary rod designer, Dawn Holbrook. In 1972, as part of a Washington Fly Fishing Club pamphlet, he recommended trying three fly types, in the following order, until meeting with success. (1) chironomid, (2) damsel nymph, and (3) mayfly. He also divulged a very practical tip: The method of presentation is more important than fly pattern selection.

I like to drift or mooch along the shoreline areas at Pass in either a boat or float tube until fish are located; then exploit the discovered location with direct casts and retrieves. It is imperative, especially when moving at a slow speed, to twitch the fly slightly every thirty seconds. When presenting a fly at "dead drift" from an anchored boat, try retrieving it gingerly, just an inch or so, and your hook-ups will increase dramatically.

On a perfect May evening, the wind will bring about a rippling effect to the lake's surface. This is a preferable condition to that of flat, glassy water because the fish are a bit more aggressive to the artificial. The moving water seems to disguise the imitation, which blends right in with the natural insects. Try casting an appropriate dry or soft hackle fly near the north end of the lake for fast surface activity at dusk.

When summer heat descends upon the lake, vegetation blooms make fishing more difficult, so most anglers patiently wait for cooler temperatures. Late Fall can be a great time to visit again — when large streamers and leeches take their share of fish.

As for Winter, our Fly Club has had outings at Pass in February, but I shall never again float tube in a lake that cold. I think a dozen of us caught only one small fish, total, the whole day. Stormy Winter weekends are better spent tying flies or cooking clam chowder — not lake fishing with the fly.

Due to it's location within a State Park, Pass Lake seems to have a bright, well protected future as trophy trout water. Over a period of five decades, hundreds of angling fledglings have received their indoctrination to the long rod at this granddaddy of all fly-only lakes. As soon as they are older, my children will go there too. Naturally, we will need a bigger boat by then. And when one of them asks; "Dad, why are you using that silly blue fly?" I'll have to say — "I can't explain it now, but would you please hand me the smoked salmon."

Those Who Came Before

I believe it was Sparse Grey Hackle (Alfred Miller) who once said that "some of the best fishing is in print." With regard to angling opportunities in the Northwest, at the time of this statement, it would be difficult to concur because fishing was just too good back then. Compared to present day fishing prospects in our region, the printed word in books and magazines might be more alluring.

I, for one, am still pleased with Washington's angling resources and manage to find good sport throughout the state, all year long. But there is no denying the fact that a fishing book or two can keep the piscatorial fires aglow during a lingering January snow storm.

While there are, currently, hundreds of interesting fly fishing titles from which to choose, a new generation of anglers can discover older or out-of-print fishing literature describing early aspects of our hobby — an angling heritage that provides a foundation for all that is fresh and innovative.

Early angling writers seem to possess a sensitivity, almost a naiveté hard to duplicate in our modern, ultra-pragmatic society.

The aforementioned "Mr. Hackle", for example, expressed universal sentiment in his short story *The Indomitable,* a tearful tribute to a proud, World War One veteran bearing only one arm with which to cast a fly (<u>Fishless Days and Angling Nights</u>, 1971).

On a lighter note; another easterner, Odell Shepard, took satirical aim at those who would claim angling was a cruel practice. In the scarce 1930 masterpiece, <u>Thy Rod and Thy Creel</u>, he humorously relates an old English yarn about a trout family and their reoccurring tragedy as members of the clan are mercilessly pulled from their watery home and harassed by sadistic fishermen.

Our own region, The Northwest, carries with it a sizable array of quality fly fishing literature. At the forefront of this esteemed library are the books of Roderick Haig-Brown. Beginning with animal and nature subjects in his first books

Silver, Pool and Rapid, and Panther, Haig-Brown eventually obtained publication of the Western Angler at Derrydale Press in 1939.

Although this monumental work was about fishing in neighboring Canada, much of the information was valid to anglers south of the border — and it set the tone for things to come. Over the next thirty years, Haig-Brown delivered time and again with visionary themes and poetic interpretations of the landscapes and waterways in the Northwest region.

His famous "seasons" books (Fisherman's Spring, Fisherman's Summer, Fisherman's Fall, and Fisherman's Winter), illustrate an angler's affection for and connection to different fish species and the environment man shares with them. All four books are steeped in literary worth. Since fly fishing knowledge is expertly dispensed throughout, these books have developed a strong following in angling circles the world over. Their popularity continues to soar.

A more obscure Haig-Brown work, Measure of the Year, is considered by some to be his best. My copy is the 1950 Canadian edition published by Wm. Collins Sons & Co. Not a fishing book; the bulk of the autobiographical narrative explores Haig-Brown's life from month to month on the north end of Vancouver Island, in a rural setting that becomes the fantasy of any reader yearning for a simpler life.

Another unusual Haig-Brown book is <u>Return to the River</u>, the scientifically correct and emotionally stirring account of a chinook salmon from birth to unavoidable, instinctive death. As the salmon travels between natural and human generated danger, we are drawn into the fish's world and Haig-Brown's exceptional story line — which suggests that readers explore some of their own feelings. The reader becomes wholly enamored with "Spring" the salmon hero, knowing full-well that she will expire at the end of her journey. Truly a remarkable tale.

Ask a Haig-Brown fan which book is their favorite and nine times out of ten the answer will be <u>A River Never Sleeps</u>, probably the most prophetic and poetic piece of literature ever created about fly fishing in moving water. For that matter, <u>A River Never Sleeps</u> could be simply the best outdoor book of all time.

An excellent way to enjoy the pinnacle of Haig-Brown's writing along with the strikingly sharp photography of Washington's own Ralph Wahl, is to borrow or acquire a copy of <u>Come Wade the River</u>. Long out-of-print, this bound gallery of

Ralph's black and white photographs interspersed with passages from <u>A River Never Sleeps</u> is a tribute to both men.

Ralph Wahl has, for good reason, been called the Ansel Adams of fly fishing. He accomplished the developing and enlarging chores for <u>Come Wade the River</u> in his own basement darkroom. And, at Ralph's insistence, the book was printed in a large folio design on high quality enameled paper.

More of Ralph's photographs can be found in the recent <u>One Man's Steelhead Shangri-La</u>, an inviting hardbound book detailing a lifetime of fly fishing his special run on the Skagit River.

Scores of regional fishermen cut their teeth on Enos Bradner's treatise <u>Northwest Angling</u>, back in the 1950's and 60's. And anglers such as Haig-Brown, Wahl, and Bradner paved the way for us all. But it is interesting to note that some of the first fishermen to write about our region were Zane Grey (the western novelist) and Ray Bergman.

Zane Grey was notorious for his far flung excursions to fish for marlin, yellowtail, and large trout in exotic destinations like New Zealand. However, in the 1920's he traveled to fish the rivers of Oregon and Washington as documented in <u>Tales of Fresh Water Fishing</u>.

Ray Bergman was Fishing Editor for *Outdoor Life* magazine. In his ageless book, <u>Trout,</u> an entire chapter was devoted to fishing "out west" on Oregon's Umpqua River. Anglers of that time (1938) traced the footsteps of both Bergman and Grey to find out, first hand, just how good the fishing was.

And we continue to follow the footsteps of those who came before. Northwest anglers of the impending new century will, no doubt, glean much enthusiasm from authors such as Steve Raymond. Raymond is impeccable in his modern classic, <u>The Year of the Angler</u>, originally published in 1973. Moreover, his beautifully detailed <u>Kamloops</u> has led many anglers to explore the interior lakes of British Columbia.

* * * * *

These are just a few of my favorite books and stories. Unabashed, I also admire a fishing book from an unlikely source — Dr. Seuss. It is <u>McElligot's Pool</u>, the story of a boy who is told:

"If you sat fifty years
With your worms and your wishes
You'd grow a long beard
Long before you'd catch fishes."

Called a fool by farmer McElligot, the boy remains steadfast — holding on to an incredible imagination and the golden angling virtue of patience. With these two attributes he gains satisfaction in his fishing endeavors.

May your days on the water be equally rewarding and, like the boy "... who was not such a fool" after all, best wishes for a slew of good fishes.

Epilogue
Skeeters, Gnats & Chironomids
by JM Hurlbert

No fly fisher today would be caught dead on a trout lake (drowned, no doubt) without a full array of *chironomid* imitations. I have a hundred or so myself. They catch fish. That characteristic being rare enough, I tend to go with what works. When I was a kid we didn't have chironomids. We had heard of *midges* but we had darn few of them either. Midges were something that East Coast dry fly purists fished with using *midge rods.* These were rumored to be short, delicate little cane rods that cost a lot of money. The magazine articles described these rods as something that must be cast with *finesse.* We never seemed to have much money and even less finesse, so as a consequence we didn't fish *midges* with *midge rods.* What we did have, though, were *skeeters* and *gnats. Skeeters* were little tiny bugs that flew into our ears, up our noses and onto any sensitive patch of skin and bit us. *Gnats* were the ones that flew into our ears, up our noses and onto any sensitive patch of skin and didn't bite us.

I started out fishing creeks, but eventually Dad started taking us to some high mountain trout lakes. Lakes operate differently than creeks and I soon discovered that most summer evenings on lakes there would be something called a *rise*. The trout obviously concocted these nightly events to drive us crazy. The trout would get very active, jumping and splashing and generally turning the surface of the lake into a froth. We would get very excited trying to figure out what the fish were after so we could catch them. It didn't make much sense. There were no bugs around other than a bunch of tiny gnats and skeeters. Hardly worth all the excitement. Eventually we concluded it was fish calisthenics. These were sport fish and obviously intent on keeping in shape.

I discovered chironomid fishing by accident. It was, in fact, so thoroughly accidental that I didn't know I had done it for a good twenty years or so. In my early teens I came across a number of magazine articles about nymphs, a subject I found very confusing. Fortunately some of the articles were about fly fishing. I'm still confused about the other kind. Wanting to keep up with the latest innovations in fly design, I decided, at one point, that I should invent a new nymph. At the time nobody thought to look in a fish's stomach to see what it had been eating. That sort of thing was looked upon as pretty disgusting. However, inspecting the contents of a fish's stomach is commonplace procedure today and is merely looked upon as pretty disgusting. Not knowing quite how to find a nymph to imitate, I decided to create one on general principle - the principle being that if I made it simple enough, it would look like some sort of a bug that was already swimming around in a lake somewhere. If it didn't work, I wouldn't tell anyone about it and no one could add that to their list of reasons for laughing at me. That list was more than adequate already. My nymph was nothing more than a size 12 hook with a stripped peacock quill body and a whisp of brown hackle for a tail - with two whisps of brown hackle sticking out sideways at the head to imitate legs. I figured out, eventually, that I could have dispensed with the hackle whisps at the head. By some miracle, the first time I tried it, the trout loved it.

The trout were doing their usual evening thing

of turning the surface of the lake into a froth with their calisthenics. My buddy Tom and I cast our flies out into the melee. Almost immediately they were nabbed by trout - strong and active rainbow trout. All that exercise must have made the trout hungry. In fact, they were so voracious that when one came unhooked, if not too close to shore, another trout would grab hold right away! This was convenient because it saved some casting. About the third time this happened, the folks up and down the shore, busily not catching fish, began to notice the finer qualities of our characters and started to become downright friendly. Really, as we caught more fish, our spot began to assemble a crowd. The folks fishing along the shoreline of our cove, having recognized the true and shinning magnificence of our youthful characters, edged closer and closer. When our spot got too crowded we picked up our gear and ambled on down to fish a spot where some new found admirers had so recently not been catching fish. There were too many gnats and skeeters at the first spot anyway. Tom and I tried not to be smug about our success and chortled as quietly as we could. In an amazingly short time we caught our limits, one of the few times when our limits turned out to be as many as the law allowed, and picked up our fish to leave. Catch and release was like chironomids then, basically unheard of, and it wasn't something we normally did on purpose. At this point we were besieged with the inquiries of our ardent admirers pleading with us to reveal to them the secret of our success. When the burly chum closest to me loosened his friendly neck-lock enough so that I could breath, I showed them my skimpy little nymph. Thirty seven noogies and a half dozen wrist burns later, when I finally was able to convince them that the pitiful imitation I presented was not a *decoy* fly, I was released with the promise that they would be ever so grateful if I would tie and sell them some of my nymphs. They were so grateful, in fact, that once they had their own supply they would allow us within casting distance of the water during evening trout calisthenics.

I think of that weekend as the inaugural experience in my understanding of fly fishing with nymphs — an experience that only took me a couple of decades to understand. It was definitely the most fun Tom and I had that summer, except for those darn gnats and skeeters flying up our noses. . .

J. Marc Hurlbert

Contributors

Dan Homel

Dan is a member of the Northwest Outdoor Writers Association. He is the author of two other regional books about fishing; *Diary of Northwest Trout Flies*, and *Washington State Trout Fishing ~ a guide to lakes*. Dan credits his long association with the Fourth Corner Fly Fishers of Bellingham as a valuable source of knowledge and friendship — which has served well in guiding him toward new destinations with pen and camera.

J.M. Hurlbert

Marc is a master jeweler by trade. When not toiling away in his shop, he has been known to hook a respectable number of fish on the fly. Mr. Hurlbert's reputation as a naturalist and writer of good humor is wide-spread throughout Washington fishing circles.

Ariel Shimondle

Ariel is a Seattle freelance artist specializing in the pen and ink medium. Her delicate drawings can also be seen on Northwest note cards and stationery.

Ralph Wahl

Mr. Wahl is considered by many to be the preeminent fly fishing photographer of the Twentieth Century. His work has appeared in numerous magazines, newspapers and books over the past fifty years.

R. Van Demark

Dick was inspired to create the pastel cover art while fly fishing for steelhead on the Methow River under blue skies of a colorful fall day. His original artwork and prints are displayed at several fine local galleries in Whatcom County.

Journal Notes

27 August, Monday

Fishing at the quiet pool. Trout slow to the dry fly. The water is high, creating complex currents. Reach cast presentation necessary to extend a drift further than a few yards.

Had to cast over fast water to put fly into calmer "cover areas". Swift currents picked up belly of line causing almost immediate drag on the fly.

12:30 ~

Switched to a size 10 "doddsi" nymph (Green Drake). Caught one snakey kelt at 15 inches.

Being a Monday, perhaps the area was heavily fished over the weekend. Stream is pressure sensitive. Van Demark is perplexed. He has never seen this piece of water less productive.

Spent some time practicing line mending tech-

niques and curve casts. Dick's Sage 6 weight rod is perfect for this.

The mosquitoes are particularly nasty. Wore mosquito netting all day and the buggers still nailed us.

5:00 ~

Hiked back to the truck so we could move downstream four or five miles.

Where road meets river, came upon a party of bait fishing campers. Ice chest poised to receive the kill. One guy is using a spinning lure (legal if bearing a single barbless hook). The bait ban signs are very small, faded, and not conspicuously posted. Decided not to confront them or make a big deal about it. Sat in the truck and just watched.

They eventually looked-up and saw us. We must have appeared "official" in the white truck, with baseball caps and netting over our heads. The group soon packed and split, thinking we were either game wardens or a couple of weirdoes.

Hadn't intended to scare them off, but the end result saved some wild fish from the barbecue.

7:30 ~

Evening "baetis" starting to emerge, as expected. Raising a few fish to the size 16 compara-duns (olive body, olive deer hair wing, and brown hackle clipped into a "V" at base).

Last fish, at dark, nearly seventeen.

On the way home, went to that good truck stop restaurant again. Crude-oil coffee, pizza-size pancakes, and homemade hash browns.

Arrived Bellingham 2 a.m. Great trip!

DBH

Photographs